FINN WOLFHARD

FAMOUS ACTOR

Big Buddy Books
An Imprint of Abdo Publishing
abdobooks.com

BIG BUDDY POP BIOGRAPHIES

DENNIS ST. SAUVER

abdobooks.com

Published by Abdo Publishing, a division of ABDO, PO Box 398166, Minneapolis, Minnesota 55439.
Copyright © 2019 by Abdo Consulting Group, Inc. International copyrights reserved in all countries.
No part of this book may be reproduced in any form without written permission from the publisher.
Big Buddy Books™ is a trademark and logo of Abdo Publishing.

Printed in the United States of America, North Mankato, Minnesota.
102018
012019

THIS BOOK CONTAINS
RECYCLED MATERIALS

Cover Photo: Frederick M. Brown/Getty Images.
Interior Photos: Alberto E. Rodriguez/Getty Images (p. 21); Bryan Bedder/Getty Images (p. 6); Emma
    McIntyre/Getty Images (p. 5); Evan Agostini/AP Images (p. 11); Franco Origlia/Getty Images (p.
    9); Frazer Harrison/Getty Images (pp. 15, 25, 29); Justin Sullivan/Getty Images (p. 27); Michael
    Loccisano/Getty Images (p. 17); Scott Dudelson/Getty Images (pp. 13, 23); ZUMA Press, Inc./
    Alamy Stock Photo (p. 19).

Coordinating Series Editor: Tamara L. Britton
Contributing Series Editor: Jill M. Roesler
Graphic Design: Jenny Christensen, Cody Laberda

Library of Congress Control Number: 2018948439

Publisher's Cataloging-in-Publication Data

Names: St. Sauver, Dennis, author.
Title: Finn Wolfhard / by Dennis St. Sauver.
Description: Minneapolis, Minnesota : Abdo Publishing, 2019 | Series: Big buddy
    pop biographies set 4 | Includes online resources and index.
Identifiers: ISBN 9781532118043 (lib. bdg.) | ISBN 9781532171086 (ebook)
Subjects: LCSH: Wolfhard, Finn, 2002- --Juvenile literature. | Television actors
    and actresses--Biography--Juvenile literature. | Motion picture actors and
    actresses--Biography--Juvenile literature. | Musicians--Biography--Juvenile
    literature.
Classification: DDC 791.45028092 [B]--dc23

CONTENTS

ACTOR AND MUSICIAN

Finn Wolfhard is a talented actor. Many know him best for his **role** in the Netflix **series** *Stranger Things*.

The young actor is also a musician. He is in the band Calpurnia. In addition to acting and music, Finn has also written and directed videos!

SNAPSHOT

NAME:
Finn Wolfhard

BIRTHDAY:
December 23, 2002

BIRTHPLACE:
Vancouver, British Columbia, Canada

TELEVISION SHOWS:
Stranger Things

MOVIES:
Dog Days, It

FAMILY TIES

Finn was born on December 23, 2002, in Vancouver, British Columbia, Canada. He is the son of Mary Jolivet and Eric Wolfhard. He has one older brother named Nick.

Finn's brother Nick (*right*) is also an actor.

DID YOU KNOW?

Finn's great-great-aunt Rita Jolivet was in silent films in the 1910s and 1920s.

WHERE IN THE WORLD?

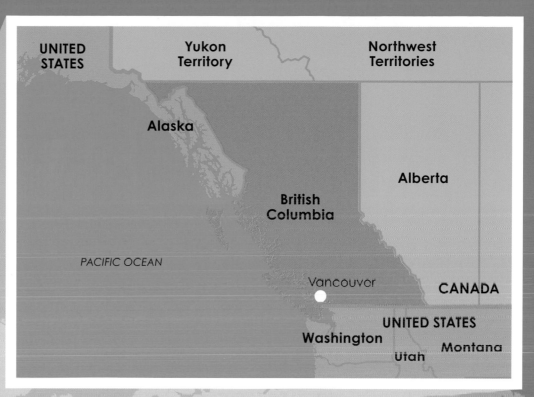

UNITED STATES

Yukon Territory

Northwest Territories

Alaska

Alberta

British Columbia

PACIFIC OCEAN

Vancouver

CANADA

UNITED STATES

Washington

Utah

Montana

EARLY YEARS

Finn showed an interest in acting at an early age. So his parents let him join an acting class.

There, his hard work paid off. He earned the **role** of Zoran in one **episode** of the TV **series** *The100*.

Finn wanted to become an actor after watching the 2002 movie *Spider-Man* starring Toby McGuire *(shown)*.

DAILY LIFE

Finn's fans love him because he is a talented and honest actor. He is a star to which fans can relate.

He goes to school each day. Then he spends time practicing with his band and hanging out with his family. His hobbies include playing video games and skateboarding.

Finn stars alongside actress Millie Bobby Brown *(right)* in *Stranger Things*. The two are also very good friends outside of acting.

Finn is very active on **social media**. He has more than 10 million followers on Instagram. And he has nearly two million followers on Twitter.

The star often posts photos with the other actors from *Stranger Things*. He also posts photos of his band Calpurnia.

DID YOU KNOW ?
Finn found his first acting role on Craigslist.

Outside of acting, Finn loves playing guitar. When he is not working or studying, he is playing guitar and singing.

STRANGER THINGS

In the show *Stranger Things*, Finn plays a character named Mike Wheeler. The show is about a group of friends living in the 1980s. The group goes out looking for their friend Will after he suddenly goes missing.

Stranger Things is moving into
its third season on Netflix.

While looking for Will, the friends **experience** mysterious events and uncover secrets. The characters in the show prove the importance of teamwork and friendship.

Finn stars alongside *(from left)* Gaten Matarazzo, Noah Schnapp, Caleb McLaughlin, Natalia Dyer, and Millie Bobby Brown in *Stranger Things*.

MOVIE STAR

With the success of *Stranger Things*, Finn was **cast** in the movie *It*. The film **premiered** in 2017. He tried out for the part around the same time he was cast for *Stranger Things*.

Finn *(top left)* played the character Richie Tozier in the movie *It*.

In 2018, Finn played the **role** of Tyler in the movie *Dog Days*. The story follows different characters through Los Angeles, California. Their lovable dogs bring them all together.

Dog Days premiered in California on August 5, 2018. Along with the actors, many dogs appeared on the red carpet that day!

MUSICIAN

Finn loves playing music with his band Calpurnia. In June 2018, the band **released** its first **EP** titled *Scout*. It featured the songs "City Boy" and "Louie."

Calpurnia **performed** in Atlanta, Georgia, and Los Angles in 2018. Both concerts sold out of tickets right away.

DID YOU KNOW
Finn was featured in four music videos before starting his own band.

The members of Calpurnia are
(left to right) Malcolm Craig, Ayla
Tesler-Mabe, Finn, and Jack Anderson.
They are all from Vancouver.

AWARDS

In 2017, Finn won a Screen Actors Guild (SAG) **Award** for *Stranger Things*. That same year, he was **nominated** for a Teen Choice Award for the Choice Breakout TV Star. And he earned three MTV Movie and TV Awards nominations.

Finn *(left)* shared the SAG Award for Outstanding Performance by an Ensemble in a Drama Series with his *Stranger Things* co-stars.

GIVING BACK

Finn truly cares about helping others. In 2016, he sold a guitar for the Sweet Relief **Foundation**. The money earned went to help musicians with health issues.

The actor also worked with a clothes company called Represent. Finn sold T-shirts to raise money to build schools in **indigenous** communities.

After Hurricane Harvey in 2017, Finn wanted to help those in need. So he sold T-shirts with frogs on them. The money went to help families in Texas rebuild.

BUZZ

Finn has appeared in science fiction, horror, and **drama** TV shows and movies. But someday, he would like to act in a **comedy**. No matter what project Finn works on, fans are excited to see what he does next!

Finn got to work with actor Sean Astin from the *Lord of the Rings* movies. They acted together on the set of *Stranger Things*.

GLOSSARY

award something that is given in recognition of good work or a good act.

cast to assign a part or role to.

comedy a funny story.

drama a play, movie, or television show that is about something serious.

EP extended play. A music recording with more than one song, but fewer than a full album.

episode one show in a series of shows.

experience the process of living through an event or events.

foundation (faun-DAY-shuhn) an organization that controls gifts of money and services.

indigenous (in-DIJ-uh-nuhs) living or existing naturally in a particular region or environment.

nominate to name as a possible winner.

perform to do something in front of an audience.

premiere (prih-MIHR) the first time a play, film, or television show is shown.

release to make available to the public.

role a part an actor plays.

series a set of similar things or events in order.

social media a form of communication on the Internet where people can share information, messages, and videos. It may include blogs and online groups.

ONLINE
RESOURCES

Booklinks
NONFICTION NETWORK
FREE! ONLINE NONFICTION RESOURCES

To learn more about Finn Wolfhard, visit **abdobooklinks.com**. These links are routinely monitored and updated to provide the most current information available.

INDEX